# MOVING IN THE RIGHT DIRECTION

## The Senior's Guide to Moving and Downsizing

Bruce Nemovitz

BOOK PUBLISHERS NETWORK

Book Publishers Network
P.O. Box 2256
Bothell • WA • 98041
PH • 425-483-3040

10 9 8

Printed in the United States of America
    First printing, October 2006
    Second printing, April 2008
    Third printing, May 2012
    Fourth printing, March 2016
    Fifth printing, December 2016
    Sixth printing, February 2018
    Seventh printing, November 2018
    Eighth printing, December 2019

    LCCN 2006933636
    ISBN  1-887542-45-0

*Editor : Vicki McCown*
*Cover Design: Laura Zugzda*
*Interior Layout: Stephanie Martindale*

THIS IS A story about four people named Everybody, Somebody, Anybody, and Nobody. There was an important job to be done and Everybody was sure that Somebody would do it. Anybody could have done it, but Nobody did it. Somebody got angry about that because it was Everybody's job. Everybody thought Anybody could do it, but Nobody realized that Everybody wouldn't do it. It ended up that Everybody blamed Somebody when Nobody did what Anybody could have done!

# DEDICATION

**I WANT TO** thank all of the wonderful folks who made this book possible by helping me to better understand the challenges and emotions involved in the moving process. Their insights, stories, and responses to my surveys taught me the importance of knowledge and understanding when helping my clients move after many years of enjoying their own home.

# CONTENTS

# IT'S HARD TO LEAVE A GOOD FRIEND...YOUR HOME!

**In talking to** my senior clients who have lived in their homes for many years, I have often thought how leaving one's home is like losing a friend. It evokes many of the same emotions.

First, there is a deep sense of loss, a void that will never be filled. Just as when a good friend departs from our lives through a disagreement, a move to another location, or death, we grieve for that person's departure. It is the same with our home. This is where we have raised our families, enjoyed good times with friends, felt personal peace and safety. It is difficult to think of replacing this "good friend" with a stranger.

Anger, too, is an emotion we often feel as we travel through this process of letting go. We become upset that reasons beyond our control have forced us to sell our life-long home—deteriorating health, financial concerns, or a changing environment are all factors that may contribute to our letting go of our treasure. We must face these emotions and deal with them in the same way we would with any important challenge.

Fear is another strong emotion that can overtake us in this process of letting go. We live in our comfort zones in our own homes; to replace that security with the unknown can evoke anxiety and stress, as we imagine every possible scenario of disappointment and heartache.

A friend sent me the following written piece that describes the loss of a friend, the reason for that friend being in our lives, and an explanation for his or her eventual departure. I believe this can apply to one of your best friends—your home!

## PEOPLE COME INTO YOUR LIFE FOR A REASON

People come into your life for a reason, a season, or a lifetime. When you know which one it is, you will know what to do for that person.

Some people come into your life for a REASON, usually to meet a need you have expressed. They have come to assist you through a difficulty, to provide you with guidance and support, to aid you physically, emotionally, or spiritually. They may seem like a godsend and they are. They are there for the reason you need them to be.

Then, without any wrongdoing on your part or at an inconvenient time, these people will say or do something to bring the relationship to an end. Sometimes they die. Sometimes they walk away. Sometimes they act up and force you to take a stand. What we must realize is that our need has been met, our desire fulfilled, their work is done.

The prayer you sent up has been answered and now it is time to move on.

Some people come into your life for a SEASON, because your turn has come to share, grow, or learn.

They bring you an experience of peace or make you laugh.

They may teach you something you have never done.

They usually give you an unbelievable amount of joy.

Believe it, it is real. But only for a season!

LIFETIME relationships teach you lifetime lessons, things you must build upon in order to have a solid emotional foundation.

Your job is to accept the lesson, love the person, and put what you have learned to use in all other relationships and areas of your life.

It is said that love is blind, but friendship is clairvoyant.

Thank you for being a part of my life, whether for a reason, a season, or a lifetime.

# ACKNOWLEDGEMENTS

**I am blessed** to have people close to me who enrich my life, both professionally and personally. My thanks go to:

My wife, Jeanne, who never let me forget who I truly am and her belief in the power of positive expression to the universe.

My daughters, Karra and Dara, who have provided love and joy.

My mother and father who have given me unlimited love and understanding and providing me with the tools to help others on their journeys.

My brothers and sister for accepting me as I am always.

My friend, Adele Lund, for offering her insights, expertise, and support as I worked on this book.

Ed Geiger, for sharing his wisdom to make this book possible.

The marketing directors of senior communities who have welcomed me to speak to the many seniors I have met. They have been a great source of information and true understanding of the challenges and concerns of seniors.

My senior clients who have shared laughter and sadness with me. Their kindness and knowledge of life have been an inspiration.

Their stories, both humorous and enlightening, have been a gift I will always cherish.

My family and friends, who have been supportive, loving, and full of wisdom and wonder. (Especially my grandson, Aidan, and his dad, Chris, who love unconditionally and never let me forget the importance of family and love of animals!) They gave me the perspective I needed to write this book and are a continuing source of laughter and joy.

All of those angels who have opened doors and pushed me through them. Without their belief in me, I would not have had the direction I needed.

# INTRODUCTION

IF YOU'RE READING this book, you are probably a senior (or know a senior) who is faced with making an important decision: whether or not to sell your home and, if you do, what kind of housing you would move into.

If you're like most people, the idea of selling your house may seem **OVERWHELMING!** You've probably lived in your home for many years, and it's filled with mementos and memories. Leaving a place that is so familiar, so comfortable, so much a part of your life may fill you with dread. Because of this, many people put off making arrangements to move from the family home, even though it no longer fits their needs and, for some, has become a burden to maintain.

In my career as a real estate professional, I have met many seniors who face this dilemma. They are usually responsible people who have invested time and money planning for their golden years, ensuring they will be comfortable and secure. However, these same people who have been so diligent in their retirement planning often leave the decision about moving out of their home to chance. They wait until they suffer an unexpected hardship that forces them to move, such as an illness or a financial setback. Unfortunately, relying upon "crisis management" to decide when to sell one's home is not only bad planning, it often leaves a person with few desirable options.

Over the years, I have worked with hundreds of seniors, helping them decide when to sell their home and guiding them to those professionals who can help them choose new housing that suits their present and future needs. This book will take you through the same process, showing you how to act proactively when making decisions about the housing you want.

As you read through the book, you may find that some of the advice will apply right now, and some will not be relevant to you for some time. That's fine. This book is meant to help you take a good look at your current situation and start thinking about how you can sustain a positive outlook and create a happy, healthy environment in the years to come. Use the book as a guide or informational resource to get you going in the right direction.

Bruce Nemovitz
Senior Real Estate Specialist (SRES)
Certified Senior Advisor (CSA)

A NOTE ON terminology: For the purpose of this book, the term "senior" refers to folks over sixty-five years old. "Senior housing" and "senior apartments" refer to housing specifically designed for those fifty-five years old and over. "Senior communities" may be independent or assisted living, life care, and continuing care communities. Definitions of types of senior housing are discussed in Chapter Four.

"YESTERDAY IS GONE, tomorrow hasn't arrived yet, but today is a gift, and that's why it's called 'the present.' Enjoy every day to the fullest—you've worked hard to get where you are and you deserve the present to be full of love and joy. And you want to take those 'presents' with you into your new home!"

# CHAPTER ONE

# WHEN IS THE RIGHT TIME TO MOVE?

AT THEIR CHURCH social, two women, Eleanor and Lois, sat together, enjoying coffee and dessert. Both were widows in their seventies. Lois had recently moved into senior housing; Eleanor still lived in her home of forty years.

As they chatted, Lois brought up the topic of her new home.

"Would you like to come over and see my new apartment?" she asked Eleanor. "How about Saturday? We could have lunch in the dining room and then play some bridge afterwards."

"Oh, no, I couldn't come on Saturday," Eleanor shook her head. "That's the day I do yard work. I can't let that go or it will just get out of hand."

"Well, what about Tuesday?" Lois suggested. "We have a guest lecturer come in the first Tuesday of every month. The last one talked about local day trips available to older people. It was really interesting."

Again, Eleanor shook her head. "I've got a handyman coming sometime on Tuesday to fix a few things. I need to be there for him, and I never know exactly when he'll show up."

Lois tried one more time.

"Well, Friday nights are movie nights. You could come and have dinner and stay to watch the movie."

Eleanor sighed. "I can't drive at night anymore, and my kids are too busy to take me places in the evening."

Lois looked at her friend with sympathy.

"It sounds like you're kind of stuck in your house. Have you ever thought about selling it and moving into senior housing?"

"No," Eleanor replied emphatically. "That might be fine for some people, but I can't leave my home. I've lived there too long to change now. Besides, I'm not ready to give up my independence."

Eleanor is not alone in how she feels about moving. Many seniors feel they just don't want to make any changes in their lives. But there comes a time for most seniors when staying in their current home is no longer a safe or wise choice. The reasons can vary. Perhaps the stairs have become difficult to negotiate. Maybe general upkeep of the house is too much to handle. A senior may experience declining health that requires more assistance and less responsibility. Or it could just be that rattling around in a house that's too big makes the person feel lonely.

Rationally, older residents may understand the reasons they should move into new, more suitable housing. Emotionally, however, many people cannot bring themselves to make the move. Because of this, many seniors continue to live in homes that do not meet their physical and/or social needs.

## Fears, Hopes, and Questions About Housing Options

As a realtor in the Metro Milwaukee area for over twenty-nine years, as well as a Senior Real Estate Specialist and Certified Senior Advisor—that is, someone who specializes in helping senior citizens make appropriate housing decisions—I have been in the homes of hundreds of seniors, listening to their stories and watching their faces. In too many cases, those faces have mirrored fear and frustration as they talked about the obstacles they have had to overcome. In our conversations, I tried to get to the root causes of their fears, hopes, and desires. I wanted to know why so many seniors stayed in their homes when it was obvious a move should be made.

The greatest mistake made by professionals working with older adults—and I was guilty of this when I first started out—is projecting our perceptions upon our clients. Because we're the professionals, we assume we know what would work best for our clients. However, I came to realize that before I could use my expertise to help my clients, I needed to fully understand them—how they thought, what they felt, and perhaps most of all, what they feared.

I decided to survey my senior clients who were still in their homes but considering moving to senior housing. Many had attended one of my "moving" seminars that provide information on affordability of senior housing, downsizing, the process of selling one's home, and moving. Most of these seniors were between ages seventy-two and eighty-three years old.

I distributed seven hundred surveys. The questions were open-ended, meaning participants were not given a choice of answers, but asked to respond in their own words. This was not a scientific study, just simply a way to gather valuable information from seniors faced with the decision to sell their home.

The following are the compiled results, including respondents' comments:

### 1. What are the top three reasons you are considering a move?

**Maintenance**            **42%**
- Home and yard too much work (can't find reliable or affordable handyman)
- Home deterioration (can't afford or are physically unable to maintain good condition)
- Snow shoveling or plowing driveway
- Responsibility of caring for a home

**Health Issues          34%**
- Will need medical help in the future
- Reduced physical abilities
- Beginning stages of dementia or Alzheimer's disease
- Can't take care of self
- Loss of eyesight

**Downsizing          10%**
- Home too large for current needs
- Kids moved out and not using space

**Loneliness          6%**
- Looking for companionship
- Someone to check on me to make sure I'm okay
- Contact with people in health emergencies
- Spouse passed away
- Children have moved out

**Transportation          6%**
- Location is not close to shopping, doctors
- Security—don't feel safe or comfortable in current surroundings
- Physically unable to drive
- Too much traffic and noise

**Age          6%**
- Getting too old to enjoy home as before

**Finances          4%**
- Too expensive to stay
- Afraid the taxes will keep going up; too high already

**Other Answers**
- Declining ambition
- Spouse doing all the work
- Need a new lifestyle
- Don't want to burden the children
- Loss of family and friends

## 2. What are the top three fears that keep you from making a move?

### Fear of Change          32%
- Moving into strange surroundings
- Going from the familiar to unfamiliar
- New setting
- Leaving the neighborhood
- Feel secure with current friends and neighbors
- Emotional separation from home
- Fear of unknown

### Fear of Downsizing      26%
- Packing and sorting is too much work
- Giving up treasures/possessions
- Where do you start?
- Entire process too difficult
- What to do with the things you won't have room for in your new home
- Physical exertion of moving

### Emotional Fears         24%
- I'll miss my home
- Will my new neighbors be compatible?
- What if I make a mistake or bad choice?
- Will I get cabin fever?
- What if I can't take my pet?
- I'm afraid I'll take too long to decide

### Financial Concerns      8%
- Monthly costs of new residence
- Income won't cover costs
- Cost increases in new residence
- Costs of moving

### Loss of Independence     4%
- Will others make decisions for me?

- I might lose control of my life
- Worried about sharing living space

**Other Answers**

- Will I have to bring my house up to code when I sell?
- My husband wants to stay and I must accommodate his wishes
- My wife has too large of a burden; she cooks, cleans, and makes decisions
- Will I like the new senior housing over a long period of time?
- Will I like community living?
- Future health concerns

### 3. How many years have you been in your present home?

- 0-20    YEARS      22%
- 21-30   YEARS      10%
- 31-40   YEARS      26%
- 41-50   YEARS      34%
- 50-60   YEARS      8%

*(Note that 68% of respondents have been in their current homes more than 30 years.)*

### 4. What do you find most confusing about current housing options?

*Respondents all mentioned cost or pricing issues. Their comments included:*

- Refundable fees vs. nonrefundable fees
- Monthly payments
- Security deposits
- Utilities
- Best options for my situation
- Poor heating and cooling systems
- Terms of lease agreement
- Rights of residents (rules and regulations)

- Anticipating future needs
- Monthly expense comparison (current vs. new residence)
- Future cost increases
- Extras, such as a pool, clubhouse, exercise room, etc., should be separate

## 5. What are the three most positive changes you see in the future?

*(Note that although the question asked for positive changes, 32% of respondents answered either in the negative or could not think of any positives.)*

**Positive**                    **68%**
- Disease control
- Medical advances
- Prescription insurance

**Negative**                    **32%**
- Can't think of anything positive
- No clue
- Won't get better/Hoping for status quo
- Everything iffy
- Future looks bleak
- We live too long
- Government is so disappointing

**Other Answers**
- Transportation improvement
- Less government corruption
- Improvement of social morality
- Enough money to last rest of life
- New friends
- Better politicians
- Trips with groups
- More done on Internet

### 6. What are your three biggest fears about the future?

**Health**                      **44%**
- Loss of physical ability
- Not able to take care of self/make own decisions
- Pain and suffering
- Burden on loved ones
- If I get sick or die before spouse, who will take care of me?
- No one to help me if I get sick/alone when ill

**Finances**                     **26%**
- Loss of financial security
- Inflation
- Can I afford change?
- Taxes are going up

**Loneliness**      *(small percentage of respondents)*
- Loss of independence
- Death of spouse
- Companionship
- Isolation
- No children—who will help take care of me?
- Alone when ill

**Government**      *(small percentage of respondents)*
- Too much government involvement
- Lack of leadership
- Safety on streets
- Federal government leading us to disaster (global ecology)
- War-war-war!
- Chemical warfare

**Other Answers**
- Making the right decision
- How long will I live?
- Not being in control, unable to drive

### 7. What have you heard most from friends and relatives who have made the move to senior housing?

**Satisfied** 76%
- Most glad they made the move
- Most seem happy
- Relief from duties at home
- Lifestyle improved
- Was a good idea
- Making new friends
- Chores and meals done for them
- Travel and have fun without worry of home
- Should have done it sooner!

**Not Satisfied** 12%
- New home too small
- Circumstances forced their decision
- Hard to adjust to downsizing
- Too much time on hands

**Not Sure/No Opinion** 12%

## What I Learned

After reading the responses, I could clearly see what kept many seniors from making a move they could or should make: **fear of the unknown**. Of course, this is simply human nature. We are all "victims" of stability, typically preferring what's familiar to the unfamiliar. Because we find it easier to do nothing, to maintain the status quo, we'll stay in situations even if we are unhappy! Look at how many people remain in bad marriages or continue working at jobs they hate. We are creatures of habit; we often choose to stay with what we know, even though it may be to the detriment of our happiness and well-being.

An old story illustrates this point well.

There once was a fox and a scorpion. The scorpion needed to get across a pond and asked the fox for a ride on his nose. The fox agreed, having known the scorpion to be honest and kind. Half way across, in the middle and deepest part of the pond, the scorpion reared up and stung the fox on the nose! The fox was startled and asked, "Why did you sting me on the nose? Now I will drown and we will both die!" The scorpion replied simply, "I stung you because that's what scorpions do."

The moral of the story is that, like the scorpion, people do what they know how to do. When it comes time for seniors to make a change in their housing, they must move from what they know to what they do not know. It may not be healthy, but the comfort and security of a known condition seems preferable to an unknown one, even though making the change would be better for their personal well-being.

## What Can Be Done?

It's understandable that many seniors fear and resist change, especially when it comes to moving from a home they have lived in for many years. The first step in overcoming the fear of moving is to talk to professionals who can assess each situation and offer the best options for health and financial needs. We'll talk more about the many people who offer services that can help in Chapter Three.

Making a move is a big event in one's life, and not a decision to be made lightly. Seniors must look deep inside themselves and

IF YOU ARE a child, friend, or caretaker of a senior, you can help by acknowledging his or her fears, talking about the situation, exploring the options, and providing reassurance that any obstacle can be overcome. Let the senior know that there are many professionals who are ready and willing to help the senior make the transition: companies that repair a home for sale, sell and pack personal property, help in arranging finances, etc.

ask the hard questions. Is their current lifestyle the one they worked so hard for their entire life? Is this the way they want to spend the rest of their life? Would a move make life easier, more enjoyable, healthier? Friends, family, and industry professionals can help seniors make the right choice.

## Summary

→ Many seniors have come to the point in their lives where a move from the family home makes good sense.

→ Seniors are often reluctant to make a move, citing fear of change and of the unknown.

→ Typically, seniors who have moved from their home to senior housing report satisfaction with their new living arrangements.

→ Relatives can help seniors make the right choice by supporting their efforts to contact professionals and accompanying them on tours of senior housing facilities.

# OVERCOMING FEAR OF CHANGE

AT THE SUPERMARKET, an older couple, Jim and Helen, ran into their friend, Marian, a widow whom they hadn't seen for some time.

As they stood in the produce section catching up on news, Jim mentioned the times their family had been invited to Marian's home when her husband, Martin, was still alive.

"You always did throw the best parties!" Jim said. "Remember the Halloween party you had one year? How you decorated your house like a haunted mansion? Our kids still talk about that."

Helen agreed. "What about that big Fourth of July barbecue, where we had sack races and a tug-of-war? And all the side dishes on the buffet were either red, white, or blue. That was a fun one!"

"You're such a great hostess," said Jim. "When are you going to have another party?"

"Oh, soon, I hope," said Marian, vaguely. "But, you know, I'm going to be doing some traveling, so I'll have to see when a good date would be."

When they parted a few minutes later, Helen said, "Don't forget to put us on the list for your next get-together!"

"Oh, I won't," Marian said with a bright smile.

What Marian couldn't tell her friends was that she would probably never have another party. After her husband passed away, Marian found herself left with the responsibility of maintaining her aging home in which she had lived for more than thirty years. Although she knew the house needed several improvements, she lived on a tight budget and did not have the resources to maintain it as she would have liked. Her home began to deteriorate, and because she was ashamed of its condition, Marian stopped entertaining. Instead of hosting parties for her friends and family members, which was her passion, Marian isolated herself and could no longer enjoy the home she had once cherished.

Although Marian felt trapped in her home, she also feared moving out, and so she simply stayed where she was and watched as her house became more and more of a liability.

## Leaving Home

Owning one's own home is the epitome of the American Dream. But as home owners grow older, the constant, sometimes back-breaking work it takes to maintain that home—not to mention the escalating costs—can turn that dream into a nightmare. As shown in the survey, while people enjoyed the privacy that comes with owning their own home, many also found the upkeep to be a hardship.

I knew of Marian's case because she had written me a letter asking for help. She knew she had to do something about her situation, but she didn't know what. When I received her letter, I called her and suggested she come to see me.

During our chat, I asked Marian some important questions:

◆ Do you have trouble maintaining your home the way you'd like to?

- Have there been health changes or restrictions limiting your ability to maintain your home, and does your home meet those challenges?

- Is this the best location to proximity to doctors, family, etc.?
- Have you cut yourself off from your friends and family because you're no longer proud to invite them to your home?
- Have you had trouble finding good workers to take care of the maintenance problems?
- Are finances keeping you from enjoying the home you've loved for so many years?

Once Marian thought about and answered these questions, it became clear to her what she should do. She made the decision to move from her home and I was able to help her sell the home and find new housing that better suited her needs.

Although Marian felt alone in her failure to maintain her home, the truth is I have seen clients suffer through Marian's situation time and time again. I always reassure them that they needn't feel ashamed; it's a fact of life that maintaining a home takes time, money, and physical ability. As people grow older they may not be able to invest either to keep up their home.

If you're considering a move, ask yourself the same questions I asked Marian to help clarify your situation. If you answer "yes" to more than one of these questions, then a change would probably be advantageous for you. Leaving your home of many years may seem scary, but the good news is that lots of cost-effective options are out there and you can find something that fits both your needs and your budget. Of course, it takes a little legwork, but there are people who can help.

## So You Think You Live in Your Home for Free...

We all put off making decisions that take us out of our comfort zone. Moving out of one's home after thirty-five or forty years would certainly cause most people some anxiety. Seniors in this situation often find reasons to avoid making the move. One popular argument I hear is that they live in their home for free.

While I can see how they may think this is true, in reality living in their own home does require some expense on their part. Utilities, taxes, insurance, and maintenance are all tangible costs of home ownership. However, another high cost that can come with home ownership—and one that is not so readily apparent—is not maximizing the power of home equity.

For example, say you have a home you've lived in for some time but are reluctant to sell. If the real estate market is flat or has a lower appreciation rate than in the past, then your equity is not working to its maximum ability. That could make selling your home now a smart move. Most homeowners will pay little or no capital gains tax when the home is sold. (Couples are exempt up to $500,000 in gain, single homeowners up to $250,000 in gain. Sellers must have lived in the home two out of the previous five years as a principal residence.) Therefore, when the home is sold, this tax-free equity can be invested to work for your independence and freedom! If interest rates do go up, you would receive higher rates of return on your nest egg.

To find out the best time for you to sell, talk to the professionals. A Senior Real Estate Specialist will help you determine how much equity you have in your home, so that you can benefit from your many years of your home's appreciation. A Senior Financial Planner will guide you in how to make that equity work for you.

Use your assets and knowledge to achieve freedom and independence that you truly deserve!

## How to Defeat Fear

As our survey showed, seniors have several concerns about moving out of their home and into senior housing. Change often brings with it a certain amount of discomfort, much of which stems from the fear of the unknown. It's understandable, even reasonable, to find change scary and difficult.

But the survey participants also saw some of the benefits of such a move. As with every choice we make in life, there are positive and negative aspects. The key is to make the choice that offers the best possible outcome for you.

The following are steps you can take to overcome the fear of change:

1) Call or visit the chamber of commerce in your town to find out the various kinds of senior housing available, such as apartments, condominiums, or an independent care community. (See resources.)

2) Visit the senior communities and senior apartments in your area. You will be surprised at the many wonderful choices. Marketing directors will be happy to give you a personal tour of their facility and explain the many different types of senior housing available—from senior apartments to retirement communities to continuing care communities. They will help you analyze your financial capabilities and assess your particular situation to suggest a type of housing to match your lifestyle, health needs, and personal preferences.

3) Talk to your trusted advisors: clergy, attorney, relatives, physician, best friend. Tell them your true feelings and describe how your current situation is affecting your way of life. Divulge any difficulties you may be experiencing, such as physical hardships, family opposition, anxieties, or loneliness. Let them guide you with their love and concern and help you make the right decision.

4) Talk to your friends and family who have already made the move. Find out how they are doing, as well as what tools they used to make their decision.

5) On a piece of paper, make two lists, side by side. On one side write down all the benefits of moving; on the other side do the same with all the objections you may have. Then put the sheet away. After a couple of days or so, take it out and read your answers. By taking a fresh look, you may see more clearly the path you want to take.

6) Look for Senior Resource Guides (magazines and publications describing all of the various Senior Communities and housing options). Try the local library, senior centers, or the Internet.

7) Call or visit the Department on Aging in your area.

8) Locate a Senior Planner or Senior Placement Service in your area.

You'll find a lot of people will want to help you make the right choice.

---

KNOW THAT "FEAR" (False Evidence Appearing Real) can mislead you into feeling you have to accept a difficult situation. You don't want to let fear spoil your golden years, especially when you've long anticipated the day when you can simply relax and enjoy life!

## Summary

→ Ask yourself whether you are able to maintain your home as well as you'd like. If not, what are the obstacles you face?

→ Before deciding whether to stay or move, call for information about and take tours of various kinds of senior housing.

→ Tell friends and family about your situation and ask for their ideas or personal experiences that might help you in your decision.

→ Make a list of positive and negative outcomes of a move from your home to senior housing. Be honest with yourself.

→ Talk to your spouse or significant other to make sure you understand each other's feelings and desires.

## Why So Many Seniors Avoid Making a Move

We can always find a good reason to procrastinate, and that's especially true when it comes to making a major move in our lives. Let's look at a few of the reasons seniors put off making a decision to change their housing situation:

➤ **Too many choices**. There are lots of options available to seniors when it comes to senior housing. This is a good thing! However, so many choices can confuse people, making it hard to know where to start. It's like looking for a new car. A buyer has to consider the size of the car, color, age, gas mileage, price, and on and on. It can be overwhelming.

➤ **The wrong decision.** With all those choices, what if the wrong decision is made? A move may make life better, but how can anyone be sure they will be happy and comfortable with the choice they've made? No one wants to make a mistake and have to move twice. Seniors want to be assured that they will enjoy their new surroundings.

➤ **Downsizing.** The very thought of getting rid of all the things one has collected over the years can paralyze a person. Many people are "save-aholics," storing away this and that just in case they might need it someday. What do people do with all of the "treasures" they have accumulated over the years?

➤ **Money.** Many seniors are afraid they can't afford to make the move. They would like some kind of guarantee that their money will last and they will live in comfort for the rest of their lives.

If you find yourself putting off moving for any of these reasons, here are six steps you can take to help you overcome that procrastination:

1. **Gather as much information about senior housing as possible.** You can start by obtaining publications devoted to listing all of the housing in your area, as well as the descriptions of services, pricing, and locations for the many types of senior options available. Many magazines for senior readers offer excellent sources of senior housing information. Check the AARP Web site, your local senior centers, and the public library. These publications will also explain the definitions of the different options available.

2. **Know your personal assets.** A good start would be to obtain a market estimate on your current home, so you know the equity you possess. Call a Senior Real Estate Specialist (SRES) who will give you a free market analysis of your home. Over 45 percent of seniors consider their home to be their greatest asset. Talk with a senior planner or financial consultant to determine the monthly expenditure you can afford.

3. **Start the downsizing process now!** Even if you are not moving for two or three years or more, you can always benefit by reducing the size of your personal property kingdom. Here's a tip for getting a quick start. Buy a pack of post-it notepads that has several different colors. Each color will represent what you want to do with items you plan to get rid of:
   - ♦ blue = sell
   - ♦ yellow = give to a friend or family member
   - ♦ pink = donate to an organization or thrift store
   - ♦ green = throw away

...and so on. Go into one room at a time and stick the slips on the items you're ready to part with. On those items you plan to give to someone in particular—such as your award for the longest hot dog throw at the company picnic, which your lucky son Bob will get—write that person's name on the slip.

4. **Assess your future needs.** First and foremost—BE REALISTIC! Look at your health needs. If you can't walk up stairs, a one-level unit is essential. Transportation may be important if you can't drive and you need to see doctors on a regular basis. Look at your monthly income, so you know what you can afford. Evaluate what kind of events and socialization you'd like to take part in. Consider all of your needs and desires for a happy life.

5. **Match your needs and desires to the right situation.** If you've followed the previous steps, you know the options available and your own resources. Now you can seek the right housing to match your health, monetary, and emotional needs.

The key to beating procrastination is taking one step at a time, breaking down what seems like an overwhelming task into bite-size, easily digestible chunks. Before you know it, you will be well on your way to a happy and full lifestyle in your new home.

# CHAPTER THREE

# WHO'S IN CHARGE?

IT WAS EARLY Monday morning, and the office hummed with activity. As I sat going over some papers, the receptionist buzzed me.

"I have a Dave Johnson on the phone," she told me. "He says he's worried about his mother and needs some advice. Can you talk to him?"

I punched the button for line three and picked up the phone. I had a good idea what I was going to hear. After introducing myself, I asked how I could help. And the story poured out.

"It's my mom," Dave said. "She's a widow in her late seventies. She lives alone in the family home where we grew up, about an hour's drive from here. The house is really too big for her now, and frankly, it's starting to fall apart. My brother and I try to help her out—we mow the lawn and take care of small repairs. But we have families too, and there just isn't enough time in the day to take care of everything that house needs to have done." I could hear the anguish in his voice. "I want her to be happy. My brother and I think she would be more comfortable in a smaller place. But, every time we bring it up..." His voice trailed off miserably.

23

"She gets angry and upset?" I finished for him.

"Yep." Then I heard him chuckle. "I bet you've heard this story before."

He's right. His is a common problem, especially now that folks are living longer than ever before. Many people in their seventies, eighties, and even nineties have many productive years ahead of them, but as they age, they need more help to maintain their independence. Naturally, many rely on their children for assistance, but family members often have busy schedules of their own or live too far away to be of much help. When children suggest their parents sell the family home and move into something smaller, more convenient, and easier to maintain, the idea is often met with resentment and resistance.

While I couldn't promise to change his mother's mind, I could start a process that might help Dave's family. I suggested I stop out to his mother's home to discuss possible solutions.

## The First Step

Making a major change in one's life—such as moving out of a long-time family home—is a daunting proposition, no matter what your age. For seniors, the idea of changing everything in their lives can just seem too overwhelming, so they do nothing.

The first critical step to take in the process is to open up the lines of communication. When Dave and his mother met with me, my main objective was to give them both the opportunity to voice their concerns. Dave talked about the difficulty of maintaining the house, how he worried about his mom living alone, and that he thought she would enjoy being around people her own age. Dave's mom said she didn't think she'd find a place she'd like as well as her own house, that she didn't want to go to "an old folks' home," and confessed that the idea of having to do something with all the stuff she'd collected over the last three decades just seemed like too much work.

It also came out in their discussion that Dave's mom had some health issues and was living on a fixed income, another source of anxiety for both of them. What if she couldn't afford to live in a place where she could get the care she needed, especially as she grew older and could possibly have additional health care issues?

I assured them both that although the challenges they were facing seemed a bit intimidating, I felt confident that, with a little work, we could find a solution that would satisfy both Mrs. Johnson and her children.

## Let the Professionals Help

With the growing senior population, a whole industry of professionals has emerged to help people like Dave and his mom with their situation. Let's take a look at a few I recommend to my clients:

**Certified Senior Financial Advisor, Senior Planner, or Elder Law Attorney**: Before you can decide what course to take, you must know how much money you have at your disposal. A Certified Senior Financial Advisor, Senior Planner, or Elder Law Attorney will examine a person's entire financial situation, taking into consideration the needs of the senior. They will look at available assets, such as funds from the sale of a home, existing and future liabilities, and eligibility for programs to assist or subsidize the cost of housing..

**Senior Real Estate Specialist**: These professionals will visit the home to make a preliminary examination. A Senior Real Estate Specialist is trained to better understand the issues and dynamics an elder faces after many years in a home. They will look for problems that need to be addressed, such as those found in the basement, roof, furnace, electrical wiring, or plumbing, and recommend inspectors who can give specific directions for repairs. After examining the home, the Senior Real Estate Specialist will have a better idea of what the home is worth, given the real estate market and expenses that will be incurred. This gives home owners a clearer idea of their net assets, which can be reported back to the financial advisor. The picture is becoming clearer!

**Liquidators and Movers:** Once the house is sold and you're ready to move, you don't have to worry about what to do with all your stuff. Estate sale planners will come into the home, price the items you want sold, advertise and conduct the sale, and hand you a check at the end! Once you've gotten rid of all that extraneous stuff, professional movers will box up, move, and even unpack your belongings in your new home.

## Please Don't Sell That House!

"Our parents have decided to sell the family home," a thirty-something man complained to me one day. "It's just not fair. We kids (and we are always someone's child no matter what our age) don't want to see our childhood home sold to some strangers who have no idea of its history or the important part it played in our lives. We love that house!"

This is the case for so many of us. We just assume Mom and Dad will never sell the home that provided us security, comfort, and happiness for so many years. Inevitably, however, the time comes for a major change in our parents' lives—which means a change in our lives as well. Like any change, how we get through it will depend on the way in which we choose to view the event.

Selling the family home is a difficult action for a senior to take. No doubt the decision comes after much anguish and uncertainty. While it has been my experience throughout my career that most children of seniors put their parents' interest ahead of their own, there have been cases where I've witnessed the opposite. I've seen an adult child revert to banging his head against the wall in protest, just as he did when he was young, in response to his parents wanting to sell their home.

As your parents grow older, take time to assess their true needs. Would a move be beneficial for them? Would they be closer to the rest of the family, providing a safer situation in case of emergency? Would this new location offer services and choices they currently lack? If you put yourself in their place, would you want to stay where they are or would you want to move to a new location? Does the family home currently meet all of their physical demands? Are you willing to help with the everyday maintenance of their home, or are you too busy with your own family and home to help? These are questions you need to ask before you let your emotion run away from the reality of the situation at hand.

After you answer these questions honestly, you may find that a move is not only needed, but an immediate necessity. Once you come to this realization, instead of looking at this change as losing your childhood home, you will more likely see it as Mom and Dad getting a safer, more enjoyable, and stress-free way of life. More than that, a move out of the home may really be the only solution for the entire family. You will always have the memories of growing up, and, most important, you will have the peace of mind of knowing your parents live in a safe and healthy environment.

Change is an inevitable part of life. If it's time for your parents to move, you can help by supporting them in their choice. Together you can cherish the past and look forward to the future!

## Make It a Family Affair

Moving from a family home can be scary, especially when you don't know what you're facing. Having good communication and the right information will go a long way to reduce stress and fear for both parents and children.

Start with a family meeting. Let everyone in the family express their concerns. Next, meet with the professionals mentioned previously. Gather information, discuss the options, think about what works best for everyone. Take your time, if you can. Consider the feelings of all involved. In the end, your love for each other will be the source of strength and courage you need to work through this challenging process.

Taking the process step by step will make it more manageable. Oddly enough, this often becomes a time when families grow closer together. By doing the necessary legwork, researching information online and by phone, and accompanying their parents as they look at different facilities, children feel good about helping their parents through the process. And the parents get the gift of realizing how lucky they are to have kids who care about them.

In some cases, there may be sibling disagreements or misunderstandings. In these cases, it may be advisable to seek a qualified third party to advise the family members such as an elder law attorney or senior planner.

## Summary

→ Get the family together to discuss the concerns of both parents and children. If possible, start the process early and take your time researching options and deciding what to do.

→ Look into finding professionals who can help you through each step of the process. Start with a Certified Senior Specialist, Senior Planner, or Elder Law Attorney and a Senior Real Estate Specialist.

→ Everyone in the family can help, whether it's doing research online, making phone calls, or going along on visits to facilities. It can be a great opportunity for families to grow closer together.

C
H
A
P
T
E
R

F
O
U
R

# SO MANY CHOICES

EDMOND AND LUCILLE, two lively octogenarians, came to see me.

"This is Lucille's idea," Edmond informed me at the beginning of our meeting. "She thinks we ought to move. But I don't want to. We're used to our house. We're comfortable there."

"Comfortable!" Lucille retorted. "You call being cold all winter comfortable? That house is drafty because the siding needs to be replaced. And what about the electrical wiring? It's so old we blow the circuit breakers whenever we plug in a space heater."

Edmond shifted uneasily in his chair.

"Well, we've lived there so long I just don't think I'd be happy anywhere else," he complained. "Besides, where would we go?"

Lucille looked at me anxiously.

"I do worry that we won't be able to find something nice that fits our budget," she said. "And there are so many different types of places to consider. I admit, it seems too difficult to try and find something we'd be happy with."

Edmond and Lucille's complaint is one I hear frequently. Trying to find the right senior housing can seem like a daunting task. But it doesn't have to be. The information presented in this chapter will give you a good foundation before you go out and look for new housing.

## What Suits Your Needs?

Before you make a decision about moving, you will want to investigate the different types of housing available to you. Thanks to a growing senior population, a number of housing choices have been developed to accommodate a wide variety of needs.

Take your time in deciding what's right for you, giving consideration to a number of factors. Starting on page 38, you will find a series of questions that will help you assess your situation. I urge you to take a few minutes to answer these questions—and any others that might be specific to your situation. Once you've done that, you'll have a good idea of your needs and abilities and will be ready to investigate housing options.

## TYPES OF HOUSING

The following are some of the types of senior communities you may find available in your area:

### Condominiums

Condominiums are typically a single-family dwelling that offer the benefits of home ownership without the burden of upkeep. "Condos," as they are called, are set up as a complex of units; while each unit is individually owned, the entire complex is governed by an association. Condo owners pay a monthly association fee, which covers the ongoing maintenance of the entire complex. These fees can range anywhere from $80 to $500 per month (higher in some cases), depending on the square footage of the condo, the location of the complex, and the services covered. When extensive improvements are needed, the association may assess additional fees to each owner, although there is typically a reserve fund for such repairs.

Condos come in a variety of designs and with various restrictions. Some are single-level, side-by-side ranch units with attached garages; others are similar to apartments, located in a high-rise building with an elevator and underground parking. Some condo associations may restrict the age of its residents—for example, all residents may have to be at least fifty years of age. Others may not allow pets or if allowed restrict type and size.

Seniors who enjoy owning their own home, but want to be relieved of the maintenance that comes with home ownership, may find condo living perfect for their needs.

## Senior Apartment Complex

A Senior Apartment Complex provides housing that caters exclusively to older adults. Residents do not own their unit, but pay rent, usually on a monthly basis. This type of housing suits those who are still able to care for themselves, but who cannot or do not want to own their own home. Typically, services offered in these housing communities are limited, as residents are assumed to still be able to take care of their own needs.

## Retirement Community

A Retirement Community is a self-contained residential development designed for older adults. Though most offer apartment-style living, a few also offer a condo option within the community. You can expect to find amenities such as a convenience store, bank, library, chapel, fitness equipment, and beauty and barber shops. Dining services can vary in the number of meals offered daily, the number of meals required, and the ease and flexibility with which you access them. Lifestyle programming may offer numerous activities within the facility, such as card games, bingo, book clubs, and religious services, as well as outings, to the theatre or to a restaurant. Shuttle buses can provide transportation to area grocery stores, malls, area shops, and more, making it convenient to accomplish your errands without having to drive your own car.

If the time should come where your health needs change and you require a little help in the course of the day, retirement communities also offer assisted living services. Help with dressing, bathing, and medication monitoring, in addition to the social and recreational programming previously mentioned, all allow for a good quality-of-life experience. The level of medical services can vary from one community to the next, with some even having specially trained staff and facilities to meet the needs of those individuals diagnosed with dementia. Because of the vast difference in staffing and services in communities, it's important to ask a lot of questions when you visit. Overall, the goal of assisted living is to provide you with the support and care you need to lead as independent a life as possible.

> WHEN YOU FIND a facility you like, ask about availability, even if you're not ready to move just yet. If it has a waiting list, it's a good idea to get on that list well before you plan to move. Then, don't wait too long. Make the change while you have your health and can enjoy your new home.

## Continuing Care Retirement Community

This community has all the same features as the Retirement Community described above. In addition, it also has its own skilled nursing facility on the same campus. As health needs change, a resident would have the ability to move through the various levels of care without leaving the campus.

Continuing Care Retirement Communities offer three levels of living:

1. Independent

2. Assisted Living - including Community Base Residential Facility (CBRF) and Residential Care Apartment Complex (RCAC)

3. Skilled Nursing Facility ( Nursing Home/Health Center)

By providing these different levels of service, personnel at continuing care facilities can adapt the type of care for each resident as health changes occur. This relieves the burden of having to look for new housing as residents grow older and their physical needs change.

## Life Care Retirement Community

These facilities fall into the category of Continuing Care Retirement Community, but are distinctive in two ways:

1. By virtue of paying an endowment/entrance fee along with a monthly service fee, you have limited the cost of any future assisted living or nursing home care you may need. The entrance fee is typically refundable for a limited time (amortized over three to five years).

2. Residents are given guaranteed placement in their skilled nursing facility (SNF).

A recent study has shown that residents in assisted living with a full-time registered nurse (RN) have less than 50 percent chance of moving to a nursing home when compared with other facilities staffed differently. When considering an assisted living facility, it is important that you understand the level of staffing and skill of those who are providing the care. Don't be afraid to ask questions!

## FEE STRUCTURES AND COSTS

As many variations of housing options there are, you'll find an equal number of ways in which the fees for those options are structured. Entrance fee versus no entrance fee. Packaged services versus à la carte. Which is the best? There is no single right answer, but the following information will help you find the right answer for you.

## Independent

Some facilities require an entrance fee (also known as an endowment fee), while many do not. If you choose a community with an entrance fee, you'll want to ask whether it is fully or partially refundable or nonrefundable. When trying to determine how large a fee you can afford, a general rule of thumb is that your assets should equal a minimum of two times the entrance fee.

If you choose a facility with no entrance fee, you'll typically be asked to sign a one-year lease, pay a security deposit equal to one month's rent, and then pay your monthly rent on an ongoing basis.

## Assisted Living

Most assisted living facilities do not require an entrance fee. Your cost here is based upon the type of housing and size of apartment you reside in, added to the level of services and care you require. The cost of care can vary significantly, depending upon how much staff time you require as well as who needs to provide that care (for example, an aide versus a registered nurse). Some communities will offer service packages; others will use an à la carte approach, and still others will have some variation of both. What most consumers should look for are a facility's ability to administer the services needed, along with the ability to adjust those services as health needs change—yet have a somewhat consistent expectation of what the monthly cost will be. Though significant health changes can reasonably result in higher costs, the little adjustments most people experience over time as they age should not cause a wholesale change in their budgeted expenses. With the average length of stay for an assisted living resident being about two years, it's important to have a handle on expected costs.

## Nursing Home

Much of the care that historically could be given only in a nursing home setting can now be accomplished in an assisted living facility for a lesser cost. With that in mind you'll find that fewer older adults need nursing home care, and those who do are typically finding their stay to be much shorter than just five years ago. Though their position in the health care system is changing, nursing homes still play an important role in rehabilitation and working with people who have chronic and unstable health conditions.

Okay, you've answered the questions about your housing needs and you know what kind of housing is available. What's the next step? Get out and tour some communities. You can collect literature, you can review all the glossy flyers, but when you tour, you begin to feel the personality of the community. Meeting the staff and visiting with other residents will give you more in an hour than you can gather over years through the mail. Ask a friend or family member to go with you to tour your potential new home. On-site housing managers or marketing directors will be happy to show you around and answer your questions.

Those clients of mine who have made successful moves are the ones who did the most advanced planning and research, along with visiting numerous communities. However, there is one factor you should take into consideration—one you can't plan for, but is important all the same: your gut feeling. When you walk into a place and it doesn't "feel" right, that's your intuition talking. Listen to it. As the saying goes, "Know thyself." If you do your homework and trust your instincts, you will find just the right housing community that fits your personal needs and desires.

# QUESTIONS TO ASK
## WHEN CONSIDERING A MOVE:

Questions about you:

❖ Goals and priorities
  ◆ Why are you considering making a move?
  ◆ What are you looking to accomplish by making a change?
  ◆ What goals have you set for the short term? For the long-term?

❖ Financial Concerns
  ◆ What are your assets and income?
  ◆ How much can you afford to pay for housing?

❖ Physical Needs
  ◆ Do you have any limitations?
  ◆ What kind of medical assistance do you require?

❖ Living Space
  ◆ How much room do you need?
  ◆ Do you have a pet? If so, does that affect your living requirements?
  ◆ Do you need an extra bedroom for relatives and friends who might visit?
  ◆ Since many communities have numerous public spaces for you to use, such as lounges, libraries, coffee shops, etc., would a smaller apartment suit your circumstances as well as your budget?
  ◆ Do you need one-level living or would stairs give you a chance to get some exercise every day? If you choose an apartment on an upper floor, is there an elevator in the building should your physical needs change?

❖ Social Issues
  ◆ What kinds of hobbies or social activities do you enjoy?

- Do you look forward to meeting new people when you move into a housing community?
- Would you enjoy participating in organized activities and socializing with other residents?
- Does the community social calendar have activities that match your interests?

❖ Day-to-Day Living
- How important is your privacy?
- How much help do you need with daily living, such as fixing meals, doing housework, bathing, etc.?
- Can you drive yourself to do your errands or do you need assistance getting around?

*Periodically review your priorities, needs, and desires. As your knowledge increases, you may find yourself needing to ask different questions.*

Questions about the facility and staff:

❖ Services
- What kind of services do they offer?
- Are they flexible in their services?
- Should your needs change, will you be able to stay in your current housing unit, or will you need to move to another location either within your community or in a different facility?

❖ Health Care
- What access to health care does the facility offer?
- Is there a medical director with on-site office hours?
- If it's an assisted living facility, does it have a full-time RN on-site?

❖ Admission Procedures
- Is there a waiting list and does it require a deposit?

- ◆ Is your waiting list deposit refundable if you decide not to move there?
- ◆ How many times can you decline an offered apartment without dropping down on the list?
- ◆ Do they require an entrance fee? If so, is that fee refundable? Under what circumstances would you lose any part of that fee?

❖ Reputation
- ◆ What kind of reputation does the facility have?
- ◆ How long have they been in business?
- ◆ Are they financially sound?

❖ Location
- ◆ Do you like the location of the facility?
- ◆ Is it close to your family and friends, doctors' offices, and other places you visit regularly?
- ◆ Do you feel safe in the neighborhood?

## Summary

→ Numerous housing options are available, including condominiums, senior apartment complexes, retirement communities, and facilities for continuing care, life care, and assisted living.

→ To best assess what kind of living arrangements you want, ask yourself those questions that will help you define your needs and your expectations.

→ Be sure to look at your long-term financial assets and obligations.

→ Those people who take the time to research their options are often the happiest in their new homes.

# FIX IT UP OR
# SELL "AS IS"

ON THEIR WAY to work each day, a couple drives by the same car lot, one that offers previously owned luxury vehicles. One day they see the car of their dreams: a gorgeous, shiny, top-of-the-line Cadillac. And the price displayed on the windshield is one they can afford.

Bright and early Saturday morning, they visit the car lot and excitedly ask to take the car out for a test drive.

"The Cadillac? Oh, yes, that's one's a beaut," agrees the smiling salesman. As he walks them out to the lot where the car is parked, he says, "Looks great on the outside, doesn't it?"

"On the outside? What do you mean?" they ask.

"Oh, don't worry," he reassures them. "There are a few things wrong with it, but they can all be fixed. Like the engine block. It's got a little crack, but we'll give you a credit to have it repaired."

The couple gaze at the car in dismay, their balloon of happy anticipation beginning to deflate. Still, as the salesman opens the door, they feel some of their initial excitement as they prepare to climb inside and simply enjoy sitting in the luxurious interior.

Instead, they gasp at what they see: torn upholstery, dirty carpeting, and a gaping hole where the radio used to be.

"We can't buy the car in this condition," the couple says. "Why don't you fix it up and then we'll buy it."

"Well, we could do that, but then we'd have to charge more," explains the salesman.

Their dream shattered, the couple leaves the car lot and decides to spend their money on a new, not-so-deluxe car.

Later that day another couple comes into the dealership, interested in the same car. Again, the salesman gives his pitch, making sure he divulges all of the Cadillac's troubles.

"That's okay," they say, "we can get all those things fixed. We might even put in different color carpeting. We just love this car!" They seal the deal, and the Cadillac is theirs.

The lesson learned from this story is that people often buy on emotion. A decision about an important purchase, especially one as emotional as picking the home you will live in for many years, can be based on intangibles such as sight, smell, touch—even just how the product you're buying makes you feel.

When you're ready to sell your home, you'll have some decisions of your own to make. You will need to evaluate what shape your house is in. If you have a home that looks good on the outside, but is tired and worn on the inside, that will affect your selling price as well as the length of time the home sits on the market.

Your decision to fix up your home or sell it "as is" should be based on your reason for selling, as well as the condition of your home. If you want to get the top dollar and are willing to spend some money upgrading your home to reflect contemporary décor, then spending thousands in remodeling may be for you. However, the majority of my senior clients want to sell the home they have lived in for many years just the way it is. And that is just fine!

Are there improvements that can and should be made even when selling "as is"? You bet! A few examples of problems that should be addressed are:

- a roof in need of repair (shingles are curling)
- a shifting basement wall or leaky basement
- deteriorating siding
- cracked concrete
- a faulty furnace
- old or hazardous electrical wiring
- leaky or defective plumbing

Nothing will scare away a potential buyer faster than a crumbling basement wall or a roof that needs replacing.

When you invite a Senior Real Estate Specialist to evaluate your home, he or she will point out potential problems that catch the eye, such as a crack in the basement or siding that has degraded. The Senior Real Estate Specialist may also determine other areas of concern just by chatting with you. Best of all, when and if you decide to have work done, the Senior Real Estate Specialist can recommend several reliable contractors—professionals who have demonstrated good workmanship at a fair price. By getting an honest and objective opinion from a real estate expert, you will be better prepared when making important decisions, such as whether to replace or repair a significant defect before offering your home to the public.

I had a client, Anna, who called me one day, saying she had decided to sell her house. We scheduled a time I could come over and take a walk-through. While the house was in fairly good condition, one concern I noted was a horizontal crack in the basement, with possible wall movement. From my experience over the last three decades working with housing codes, I knew the standard in the industry is a one-half to three-fourths inch of movement in a basement wall. I also knew this crack could be indicative of other problems, such as drain tile issues and drainage problems. Visible water stains told me there could be damage from mold problems. Many times folks don't feel there is any problem if the basement doesn't leak. However, a damp or dry basement can have structural wall problem. One or more of the walls may have shifted without any leakage at all!

I recommended that Anna contact an expert, and I gave her the names of contractors and structural engineers I had used previously. I knew these people would be able to determine whether there was a problem and, if so, advise her whom to contact for estimates on repairing it. If no significant problem was found, then Anna would have a report from a respected expert she could provide to potential buyers to allay their concerns.

If a structural defect is found in your home, should you fix it before putting the house on the market? If you have the funds available, I usually suggest that you do so. No buyer wants to buy a problem. A defect will distract a buyer from focusing on the positive points of your home. Instead of talking about the character and unique qualities of the home, you'll be trying to explain away a problem. Remember that buyers will always err on the side of caution. In their head they'll be doubling or tripling the cost of fixing a defect. Better to have the work done and show the prospective buyer that you have properly taken care of the problem. Most respected contractors will also include a guarantee in writing which is transferable to the new buyer. You have turned a serious problem into a positive windfall for the buyer.

When it comes to more cosmetic changes, such as replacing old carpeting, I suggest leaving things as they are. You may go to a lot of trouble and expense to put in new carpeting—only to have the new owners rip it out and put in hardwood floors. However, if you want top, top dollar, then go all the way! Don't replace carpet without painting the walls and updating the kitchen and bathrooms. But be sure to take into consideration the type of neighborhood you live in and what you can reasonably expect to sell your home for. You don't want to put a lot of money into your home if you won't be able to recoup those costs when you sell it. Again, a Senior Real Estate Specialist can help you with making those decisions.

## Don't Sweat the Home Inspection!

When I give seminars on the entire home selling process, the one topic people seem most interested in is home inspections. Home inspections have become a critical part of the real estate transaction.

When I started as a fledgling realtor in 1977, real estate agents and, consequently, home buyers relied almost 100 percent on the seller's word as to the quality and soundness of their home. There were no condition reports, as is required by law today (with certain exceptions).

A condition report asks the seller questions about any problems they may have experienced over the years with the structural and mechanical condition of the home. Questions are specific, such as "Have you had any water coming into the basement?" The real estate agent listing the property interviews the seller as to the condition of the furnace, plumbing, roof, electric wiring, foundation, siding, and other important structural properties of the house. If the seller has experienced any problems with the home or has any reports from inspectors or contractors pertinent to the condition of the home, this information must be disclosed to any potential buyer who views the property. In turn, the buyer must sign this report when an offer is made.

The purpose of the condition report is to force the seller to disclose any prior conditions about the home, especially those that might not be easily noticed. This actually works to the benefit of both the seller and the buyer, for the following reasons:

1) The buyer is made aware of any potential problems that might occur, based on the history of the house.

2) The seller is protected by this disclosure, as long as all statements are truthful so the buyer cannot claim any misrepresentation of the home.

While the condition report may seem to favor the buyer by disclosing any problems with the property, it also helps the owner.

Informed buyers are less likely to back out of an offer if they are not met with unpleasant surprises.

In some cases, a condition report may not be available, such as with estates where the seller may not be able to answer the questions due to state of mind or in cases where the seller has passed on. In these cases, buyers must rely on their own inspections.

Once an offer is accepted, the buyer typically has ten days or so (depending on what is agreed upon in the offer to purchase) to have the home inspected for major structural defects, such as basement wall and drainage issues, electrical violations, plumbing problems, and roof damage. If a defect is found that the buyer was not aware of, then the seller and buyer can negotiate and come to an agreement as to how to remedy the problem.

In my state of Wisconsin in the offer, the seller either has the right to repair any defect in a workman-like manner without the buyer having the option to back out, or the seller does not have the right to remedy the situation unless the buyer and seller can agree on a solution. If a significant defect or defects are found, I would suggest that the seller get a reputable contractor to examine the defect in question. Then both parties can view the various reports and come to an agreement on the best remedy for the situation. Many times it is settled with a dollar figure agreed upon by both parties, which can be reflected by a price reduction or simply a credit at closing to the buyer. The buyer then accepts the responsibility for making the repair. In some cases, the buyer or buyer's lender may require the defect to be rectified prior to closing. If the weather does not allow for the repair to be done prior to closing, then an escrow can be established for the repair to be done in the future with an agreed deadline. In many cases, the escrow amount can be one and a half times the estimate(s) with the excess funds returning to the party that escrowed the funds after the work is completed.

The best thing about the use of a condition report and buyers' inspections is that they keep the sellers and buyers out of court! In 1977, when I began my career, it was not unusual for a buyer to sue a seller after the closing of the sale, due to a lack of disclosure by the seller regarding defects, notices received about future assessments, repairs to streets or sidewalks, and other pertinent information that would have affected the terms of the sale.

Honesty is always the best policy, and nowhere is that more true—and important—than when it comes to selling your home. Full disclosure will make the transaction go more smoothly, keep you out of court, and give you peace of mind.

---

## WHY PURCHASE A HOME WARRANTY?

When selling a home, offering this policy can lessen the anxiety of a purchaser especially if your home is older or in need of near future repairs.

Prices to purchase a home warranty service contract range from $385-$500 for a single family residence or condominium. Multi-Families can range from $550-$750 with additional cost for each unit beyond two. These policies usually cover heating, plumbing, electrical systems, as well as major appliances, and water heater for a one year period after the date of purchase. Multiple years can be purchased for an additional cost. There can be a small deductible charge to the policy holder.

You can locate a reputable Home Warranty company by calling your local real estate agent or going to the internet searching under "Home Warranty" or see page 75 in the Resources section.

# PRESENTING YOUR HOME AT ITS BEST

When it comes time to sell your home, you want it to look as good as it possibly can. Here are some tips on how to make your home its most attractive, both inside and out:

Interior:

» First and foremost, clean up the clutter. You want the buyers to be able to focus on the house, not your belongings.

» Keep the house as clean as possible at all times. You never know when someone will want to drop by to see it.

» Create a welcoming mood in your house by turning on lights in several rooms. Pleasant aromas, such as those from candles or something delicious baking in the oven, make prospective buyers feel at home. Fresh flowers always add a touch of elegance.

» Consider getting rid of furniture that's worn or no longer needed.

» To really give your house eye-catching appeal, you can hire a company to "stage" your home. These decorating professionals know how to present your home at its best, whether it's by simply rearranging existing furniture or bringing in additional furnishings.

Exterior:

» Keep shrubs pruned and the lawn mowed. Pull those weeds before they get too big. An attractive yard indicates that your home has been well cared for.

» Power-washing cement driveways will remove oil, rust, and other stains. Patching cracks in an asphalt driveway will prevent water seepage and further cracking.

> » Compare your home to others in the neighborhood. If the paint is faded or peeling, consider applying a fresh coat.
> » Window boxes, flower pots, and planters add beauty and style to an entrance or patio.
> » Inexpensive vinyl shutters will add more dimension to exterior windows. And keeping those windows crystal clear adds brightness and conveys a sense of cleanliness.

## Summary:

→ Before you list your home, ask a Senior Real Estate Specialist to evaluate it for possible problems and give you recommendations on reputable contractors.

→ Selling your home "as is" is a viable option and sometimes even your best course of action, particularly in cases where the personal representative has not lived on the property, the seller is not living in the home anymore, etc.

→ If possible, fix the structural defects. If funds are not available to repair the major problems, then get estimates and reports from reputable experts who will be respected and believed by buyers.

→ Being upfront and honest in representing the condition of your home will help you sell your home at the right price, in a timely manner, to satisfied buyers. You'll have a better chance of completing a mutually beneficial transaction and staying out of court!

# CHAPTER SIX

# MOVING ON

**BILL AND SARAH** were a delightful couple who had decided to move into a senior apartment. They were responsible, capable people who had always done everything for themselves and took pride in their self-reliance. So when it came to dealing with forty-five years' worth of "treasures," they naturally wanted to do the sorting and packing themselves. However, because I knew their health was failing, I suggested they get some help.

"You know, packing up all your things will be pretty strenuous," I said. "I'd be happy to give you the names of some companies that specialize in helping people in your situation. These professionals can do everything—organize, pack, move, even sell your personal property."

Bill put a hand up to stop me.

"Thanks for your concern, but no, Sarah and I have always done for ourselves. We plan to do all the packing and moving on our own."

Still worried that they didn't know what they were getting into, I asked, "What about your kids? Would they be willing to lend a hand?"

"They've offered," said Bill, "but we've never been a burden on our children, and we're not about to start now. We'll be fine."

But they weren't fine. One of them developed serious back problems and both suffered from depression, and they nearly ended up in the hospital. Their frustration with their health problems turned to anger at having to move at all. They became difficult to deal with when negotiating the sale of their home and they resented the buyers for forcing them into such a situation. The whole experience deteriorated into one long nightmare.

## I Can Do It Myself!

Like Bill and Sarah, many of my senior clients are very independent, proud of their ability to take care of whatever problems arise in their lives. Several of these folks lived through the Depression years, when they learned to survive by becoming self-sufficient. Such self-reliance is a wonderful quality and one that has served them well throughout their life. However, as they become older, this philosophy of "I can do it myself" often becomes a health risk, both mentally and physically.

If you are the type who prefers to do everything yourself, I hope you will learn from Bill and Sarah's experience. Before deciding to do any downsizing yourself, take inventory of your physical limitations, such as problems with balance or high blood pressure, as well as issues concerning your back, neck, knees, heart, and lungs. Consider these questions:

❖ Can you stand and bend for long periods of time?
❖ Can you lift heavy boxes and awkward items?
❖ How long will it take you to get through the task?

Keep in mind that the real estate market has peaks and valleys. I've seen too many clients take longer than they anticipated to clean out their house. When they were finally ready to sell, the peak had passed and they found it hard to attract a buyer during the slow season, which could potentially cost them thousands.

ONE OF MY treasured senior friends made me laugh with this observation: "The older I get, the better I was!" That joke rings true for many of us as we age and forget we've acquired a few limitations along the way. Carefully evaluate just how much you want to do when it's time to downsize your possessions.

## Whom Should I Believe?

One of the most frustrating experiences I've had over my twenty-nine years in the real estate business has been dealing with the misrepresentation of facts regarding the strength or weakness of home sales. Many of us turn to our trusted newspapers to feel the pulse of the market so that we time the sale of our home to get top dollar, yet what these publications report is often inaccurate.

The real estate market—just like most other commodity markets—is subject to ebbs and flows dependent on many factors. On many occasions, the market has slowed down by 30 to 60 percent in a matter of weeks, sometimes days. Weather often plays an important role in these fluctuations, especially in those areas that experience cold winters. In the Midwest, where most of my clients live, the best months to sell are typically April, May, and June. After school lets out for summer break, we see a slow down, then an increase in activity when school resumes, from September to November. The months of December through March tend to be the slowest of the year.

Why are these patterns so important to you, the home owner? Because more buyers in the market means you will likely receive a higher price for your home as well as experience a shorter selling period.

Unfortunately, home sales reported in newspapers are based on home closings. That means when you read "real estate sales have set records for the month of July," they are referring to sales that actually took place one to two months earlier. It may be that July was in reality slow for new sales, but the statistics cited in the paper make July seem like a boom month.

If you want to find out the real trend in home sales, contact a real estate professional or real estate appraisal service. You will get invaluable advice, such as:

♦ an accurate assessment of the best time to put your home on the market
♦ a true read as to the present conditions of the market place
♦ statistics of the current year compared to last year's sales
♦ trends, both hot and cold, in the current housing market

This kind of information and guidance will help you get the best price when selling what is probably your most valuable asset—your home.

## What to Do With All That Stuff!

I hear one word over and over from my senior clients when they imagine what it will be like to downsize after so many years in their home: *overwhelming!*

After talking with hundreds of seniors at my seminars, I've learned that deciding what to do with all their "stuff" is a real challenge for seniors contemplating making a change. My survey showed "downsizing" running a close second to "fear of change" when it came to reasons why seniors didn't want to move. Comments from respondents of my survey included the following concerns: packing and sorting, giving up family treasures, starting the downsizing process, worrying about physical exertion from moving, and deciding what to do with all of their belongings.

Take "baby steps!" You took thirty, forty, fifty years to accumulate your personal belongings. Give yourself some time to find a new home for all of these things. Make it easy on yourself by following a simple strategy.

First, divide personal property into five categories:

- The first category consists of things you absolutely want to take with you. These are items you will not part with and will fit in any apartment.

- The second category contains items you may take with you depending on the size of your new home. Since you may not know the exact square footage of your new condominium or apartment, you may not want to decide where these items will go until you find your new residence.

- The third category are items you want to sell at an auction or estate sale, or donate.

- The fourth category contains items you want to give to members of your family or friends. Put a label on each item with the name of the person you feel would want that item. (Don't be disappointed if they decline to accept!)

- The fifth category—you guessed it—is everything to throw away. There are disposal companies who will bring a dumpster if necessary to dispose of these items.

Appliances usually go with the sale of your home. In many cases, buyers are coming from apartments and do not have these items. Large appliances are difficult for you to take with you and can enhance the salability of your home.

You may have valuable property that you can sell to the public. Some people hold their own estate sale, but you can also use a professional estate sale liquidator to handle the task. These companies will either buy up the personal property and take it to their showroom to sell or hold an estate sale at your home. Most companies require that the property to be sold be worth more than $4000, and they generally charge anywhere from 33 to 40 percent of the gross amount brought in at the sale. The sale usually runs for three to four days, with items discounted each day until everything is sold. The companies will typically clean the home after the sale so your buyer can move right in!

---

A REFERRAL IS a great way to find a good contractor, company, or service. Ask friends or relatives whom they have used to help dispose of their personal property. A Senior Real Estate Specialist can provide you with a list of professionals in your area that are trusted and proven to be responsible. For a list of Senior Real Estate Specialists go to their Web site at **www.seniorsrealestate.com**.

## Know What You Have!

The first step in downsizing is to know "the number." The number I'm referring to is the value of your personal property. Many of your belongings may have little or no value in today's market; on the other hand, some items may be of great value when appraised by a professional. For instance, here's a quick list of items that will bring the most money at an estate sale or auction:

| | |
|---|---|
| Gold, metals, etc. | Antique dolls |
| Jewelry | Toys |
| Model cars | Games |
| Oil paintings | Antique lamps |
| Antique posters | World War I and II items |
| Water color and other art | Ivory pieces |

Here's a more complete list broken down into different categories:

**Furniture:** Sofas, love seats, chairs, recliners, tables, cocktail and end tables, table and floor lamps, pianos, card table and chairs

**Antiques:** All furniture, fine arts, figurines, bronze or brass pieces, pewter, silver, china, glassware, crystal stemware, vases, hand-painted china dolls, clocks, sterling flatware, sterling serving pieces, silver pieces, mirrors

**Jewelry:** Costume and fine jewelry, gemstones, 14K jewelry, antique jewelry, all costume jewelry

**Arts:** Framed prints, oil paintings, pastel water color paintings, movie posters, poster prints

**More General Items:** Books—both hardback and paperback—cookbooks, records, cassette tapes, eight-track tapes, CDs, DVDs, videos, radios, telephones, frames, bar items, fireplace screen and tools, candles, plants, planters, floral arrangements, sewing machines, fabrics, yarn, office supplies, old pens, umbrellas, paper goods, gift wrapping items, perfumes, new cosmetics.

I would suggest asking your relatives, trusted advisors, friends, and coworkers if they have used the services of an appraiser for any items of value. If none have a referral to give you, then look in the yellow pages in your area under the heading "Appraisers."

There are companies that will check out the credentials of such appraisal services as well as many other service providers you may need. One national company is Angie's List. You can find Web sites for the companies mentioned here in the "Resources" section of this book.

Many cities have a number of local companies that provide this service, and I would suggest calling the Better Business Bureau to assess the credentials of these kinds of companies as well as other service providers in your area.

Before you choose a company, get two or three price quotes. When each appraiser comes to your home, make sure you let him or her know that you will be getting other opinions as to the value of your items. This will encourage them to be a bit more careful when quoting a number, and you can feel confident that you know the true value of your paintings, jewelry, or other valuable items.

You may feel that your personal property will not have enough monetary value for an estate sale company to take on the job of liquidation. If you just have furniture to sell, there are companies that will purchase every item you have and pay cash. Again, ask friends and family for recommendations on whom to contact or look in your yellow pages under "Furniture, Used."

If you want to donate items, many organizations will pick up much of your personal property. In my area, for example, there is an organization that helps battered women who need to start up in a new home setting. They have a need for furniture, dishes, linens, and other household items. For a list of organizations looking for donations of this type, you can check the Internet or ask at your church, temple, or synagogue.

Remember, there is no substitute for reliable information. Get the facts, know the value of your treasures, and then you can create a game plan to start downsizing!

> **MAKE A LIST** of those things you plan to give away and send it to your friends, coworkers, relatives, and church or temple. Put a deadline or final date to claim these items. Let them know that anything left over after the deadline will be donated to charitable organizations.

## Summary

→ Downsizing after living for decades in a home is a huge task. Before you start, take an honest look at your health and stamina.

→ Don't be afraid to ask for help from friends and family. Several professional services are available for every step of the move.

→ Make lists of those things you want to keep, give away, sell, and throw away.

# IF I KNEW THEN WHAT I KNOW NOW...

I have worked with hundreds of children of seniors, guiding them through the process of selling the home and selling and moving personal property. In a survey I sent out to these children of seniors, I received some valuable feedback:

1. What was the most challenging aspect of the sale of the home?

    *Timing between selling home and moving into new housing*

    *Cleaning out the home*

    *Doing the paperwork and knowing the various laws*

2. What services were available to assist with the downsizing of personal property?

    *Realtors used expertise to help family*

3. What would you have done differently with the entire moving process?

    *Begun process earlier*

    *Started with a lower asking price for faster sale*

    *Convinced parents to downsize sooner*

    *Asked more questions*

    *Hired company to have rummage sale*

4. When first confronted with the entire selling and moving process, what were your initial feelings?

    *Overwhelmed by huge project*

    *Incompetent*

    *Tried to make it smooth and carefree for parent*

    *Sad to sell home that had been in family so many years*

    *Worried it would be drawn-out battle*

    *Wanted to find a fair realtor*

5. What one word describes the overall downsizing, and moving process?

> *Work*
>
> *Fast*
>
> *Tiring*
>
> *Overwhelming*
>
> *Relief*
>
> *Pain*

6. How long did the entire downsizing and moving process take?

> *2 to 3 months*

7. Did your family members help in the process?

> *Yes (in most cases)*

8. If you were looking for senior housing for a parent or relative, what would your number one goal be?

> *Parents like where they will live*
>
> *Activity*
>
> *Good care*
>
> *Open communication with staff*
>
> *Clean and well-maintained*
>
> *Modern*
>
> *Let parent decide*

In summary, the children wanted what was best for their parent, but they also wanted the process to go quickly and smoothly. The best way to make this happen is to communicate and use industry professionals to help you through the process.

# LESSONS I HAVE LEARNED

**THROUGHOUT MY CAREER** in the real estate business, my senior clients have taught me much about living life. Some lessons exposed possible problems and dangers; others provided a direction or path to happiness and prosperity. I have had the opportunity to meet so many wonderful folks who have shared stories of happiness, and, yes, some of sadness. One common thread running through all of my clients is the strong urge to live a life of meaning and to feel needed by others.

I am amazed at the strength that so many possess when confronted with loss: loss of spouse, loss of health, loss of financial savings. I've often wondered how I would hold up under such challenges. One thing I do know—we all face our own challenges much better when we have a circle of family and friends to give us strength and guidance. It is so important to maintain relationships with those who care about us most. Friends and family provide the support we need to weather those tough times we all will face.

The lesson to learn? Don't go it alone! Get all of the help and support you can. Put pride aside and accept help when offered!

The happiest senior clients I have known are also the busiest. They stay connected to life by helping others and staying active. "Active" can mean traveling, volunteering, playing sports, walking, bike riding, being involved in their church, synagogue, or place of worship and much more. I realize that good health is critical to many of these activities, but even someone with compromised health can still engage in a wide variety of hobbies, continued learning, and giving help to others.

Isolation contributes to negative health issues, depression, drug and alcohol abuse, and loneliness. Staying connected to family and friends creates a sense of well-being, worth, stability, and optimism. Which sounds like a better way to live out your golden years?

The lesson here is to stay in the game of life. Keep in touch with those people who are important to you. Find ways to share your life stories with those who would love to be your friend. Don't let pride and isolation stand in the way of happiness and fulfillment.

## Wisdom Given to Me

I have been blessed with a career I love that allows me to work with people in need of my help and guidance. Throughout the many years I've been a Senior Real Estate Specialist, I have gotten to know so many great folks. And just about everyone I've met has shared a nugget of wisdom with me.

The following are some of my favorites. I think they offer good advice:

### "Don't Look Back, Just Move."

One of my favorite clients, Shirley, had a choice to make. Following the death of her husband, she knew she had to make a move. Logically, she realized she couldn't maintain the house as she and her husband used to. But, emotionally, she hated to leave her home, with all its fond memories and family history.

Little by little, Shirley started considering that she might look for some other kind of housing. Then came the day she had to pay a gardener $400 to rake and remove the leaves. That event suddenly made everything crystal clear: the time had come to move on.

"Once I decided to move, I never looked back," she says. "I kept moving forward, and even though it was a lot of work, in the end, I got rid of a lot of stuff I didn't need. Now I live in a place I love."

Shirley still has a few items she hasn't found a place for, such as her bell collection and her husband's camera, coin, and stamp collections.

"I'm in no hurry," she chuckles. "It's a work in progress."

## "Do Your Givin' While You're Livin'…"

**We are all savers**, which means when it comes time to move, we've got to decide what to do with some of that stuff.

Many seniors find it rewarding to give their treasures to friends and family. Understandably, people believe their loved ones would want to have a piece of family history or personal property that was so meaningful to them. Sometimes that's not quite true.

One story I heard from another realtor illustrates this point.

For years, Ruth collected decorative plates, which she had proudly displayed in her home. As she grew older, she anticipated the day she would move into a smaller place, and she wanted to pass on her plate collection to her children. Each month she would give away one plate to each of her two sons. She enjoyed seeing the expressions of joy when they received this precious gift, one that meant so much to her.

One day, she called her son Mark at work to tell him that she wanted to pass on her two favorite plates of the collection to him and Mike, her other son. Ruth now laughs as she tells the story.

"I was so excited!" she remembers. "I just knew the boys would love the two plates I'd be giving them that month. As it happened, Mike had dropped by to see Mark at work that same afternoon.

"'Oh,' I said, 'is Mike there too? Good. Ask him when we can all get together.'

"Well, Mark went to talk to his brother, but he forgot to put the phone on hold. In the background, I could hear Mark say, 'Hey, Mike, Mom is on the phone and she has some more junk for us.'

"My poor sons didn't want to hurt my feelings," she says with a smile. "I'm just glad I found out the truth." She took the plates back and found someone else who wanted and appreciated them.

The moral of this story is that we may *think* we know what our family or friends would like, but the truth is we really don't. And they will not want to disappoint us when they receive our treasures.

A better approach is to make a list of the items you want to give away and send this list to the people you care about. Then they can let you know which pieces of your history they would love to have. Set a deadline for them to come and take home the items they'd like or else your downsizing may never get done. One of my clients stated it more strongly: "Pick it up or you'll find it on your front porch!" He was assertive, but it worked.

So, as the saying goes: ***Do your givin' while you're livin', so you're knowin' where it's goin'!***

## "I Wish I Had Done It Sooner."

So many of my clients weren't thrilled about moving. They worried they would never find the peace and happiness they had enjoyed in their own home. As I worked with these seniors to prepare their home for sale, sell their property, and guide them through the moving process, I could see they had misgivings about the decision they'd made. Yet inevitably, two or three months after they had settled into their new community, I'd get a call.

"I love my new home! I'm socializing again. I have freedom and independence without the worry of taking care of my home. All I can say is 'Why didn't I do this sooner!'"

## "Just Do It!"

Procrastination and hesitation would paralyze many of my senior customers. Year after year I'd visit them and listen to their stories about putting off the move they knew they should make. The stairs were a challenge, driving was a problem, isolation had set in, yet they could not get themselves to begin the downsizing process and put their homes on the market. Fear of change prevented them from leaving a known situation, bad as it was, for an unknown one. What broke the cycle of procrastination? They woke up one day and decided to just do it! Like the Nike commercial (with the slogan "Just do it!"), they decided to move forward and not look back. Often that moment seemed to arrive for no apparent reason. When it did, my clients seized on it and never looked back.

## "Make New Memories; Savor the Old."

When questioned by friends about whether or not he missed his home, one resident's response has consistently been, "A house is made by human hands, but a home is made by human hearts. I have many cherished memories from the years that I lived in my home, but I have never regretted my decision to leave my house and often wish that I had made the move sooner. I have made many wonderful new memories in my new home and look forward to many more."

Another resident eloquently described the power of memories:

"When we enlist the help of family or friends, we create another beautiful memory. And, when we give away items we no longer have room for to family, friends, our place of worship, or charity of choice, we share our memories."

## Summary

→ Stay connected to the people you enjoy. Don't let isolation keep you from enjoying your golden years.

→ Keep as active as possible, mentally and physically. Activity improves health and prevents depression.

→ Seniors possess wisdom and experience worth sharing. Pass on your knowledge and memories to others around you.

# POSTSCRIPT

No matter how old you are, moving from one residence to another always brings with it a time of change and upheaval. But in the case of seniors who are leaving family homes in which they have lived for decades, their emotions can be quite complex. Everyone involved in the process—friends and relatives as well as industry professionals—can help make this transition easier and less stressful by honoring the history behind these emotions and recognizing the senior's feelings as real and valid.

As a Senior Real Estate Specialist, I have learned that the first step in helping my clients through this process is to ask questions—and then really LISTEN to the answers. Who lived in the home over the years? What were some of the highlights as well as challenging times for the homeowner? Did a spouse pass on and if so what was he or she like? Once the past has been honored, people can begin to look forward, knowing they're not abandoning their past, but bringing those important memories with them into their new life.

A move can and should be a new beginning, offering freedom and independence as well as peace of mind. I've traveled along on this journey, from beginning to end, with my clients many times. Often those first steps are tough. But I've noticed a certain phenomenon occurs over and over again. Once a new residence has been secured and the process truly begins, a fundamental shift occurs. The senior begins to look forward to a new living situation, a new life that offers so many wonderful positives. When I call a few months after the move to see how my friends are doing in their new home, more often than not I'll hear, "Why ever did I wait so long?"

The journey I've taken with my senior clients has been rewarding and highly enlightening. I have come to truly respect these people as peers and teachers. The nuggets of wisdom I've acquired from my senior clients over the years are too numerous to include in these pages, but here are a few I think are worth repeating:

> **How to live a long, happy life:** "If you want to live, keep on living! I run for political office every year. I'm ninety-nine now and hope to win this year in Congress, because I can serve until I'm a hundred-twenty years old!"

> **The best part of being over 100:** "I no longer have to worry about peer pressure!"

> **How to enjoy life:** "If you want what you've never had, do what you've never done."

> **The best way to keep a positive attitude:** "Thoughts become things, so choose the good ones."

In this book I share much of what I have learned in my twenty-nine years of working with these seniors, assisting them in "moving in the right direction." I hope you have found this book to be educational and that you use it as a starting point for yourself, a family member, or friend who is about to embark on this important and exciting journey.

Thank you for taking the time to read my book.

# COMMON
# QUESTIONS

**Q. I Made a Commitment to Rent an Apartment. Now What?!**

The following are questions that often come up after that deposit—as well as the commitment to move—is made:

**Q. Should I sell my home before my move-in date or after?**

A. This decision usually depends on your financial situation as well as your comfort level. Determine what funds will be needed to make the transition to your new apartment. Can you afford to begin your monthly payment without using the funds from the sale of your home? If so, try and allow for four to six months of payments, even though you may not need that much. It's better to allow for more payments than you will probably make; otherwise, you may find yourself being pressured into selling your home too quickly.

Also consider your personality when deciding to sell after your move-in date. Can you sleep comfortably in your new apartment, knowing your home is vacant? Some folks can; others shudder at the thought.

**Q. I know my move-in date. When should I put my home on the market?**

A. I suggest putting the home on the market sixty to ninety days prior to your move-in date if you want it to be sold before you move into your apartment.

**Q. Will my home sell better with or without the furniture?**

A. In most cases, the home will show better with the furniture. There are exceptions, such as a home that has too much clutter and nowhere for it to go or a home in which the furnishings are old and tired. However, in the majority of cases, your home will sell better and faster with furniture.

**Q. How can I avoid the stress of having to move out of my current home, close the deal, and move into my new apartment all in one day?**

A. That does sound like a problem only Houdini could solve, but, in fact, real estate professionals know how to structure an offer so the seller has time to make a smooth transition. Here's how:

Let's say your move-in date in your new apartment is May 1st. You put your home on the market March 1st. On March 2nd (Boy, that was quick!) you receive an offer to purchase from a qualified buyer. They want you to close and be out by April 15th! They might pick that date based on the interest rate they can get from their lender, who will lock in a rate for forty-five days. But that date is just too soon for you. So your agent counters the buyer's offer to reflect your wishes for a smooth transition. You agree to a closing date of April 15th, which means as of that date, the buyer owns the house. You receive full payment on that date and you are no longer responsible for taxes or maintenance of the house.

However, because you aren't quite ready to move, your agent can include a clause stating that you can stay on, as a renter or occupant in your home, until May 30th. As a renter, you will pay rent—usually the daily rate based on 1/30th of the buyer's monthly payment. If their payment is $1500 per month, then you would pay $50 per day, but only for the days that you stay, if structured this way. So, if you move out May 15th and the closing was April 15th, you pay rent for 30 days x $50 per day, or $1500. Remember, your move-in date was May 1st and your contract with your buyer allowed you to stay until May 15th, if needed. This gives you fifteen days after your move-in date at your new apartment—so you don't have the pressure of moving out, closing the deal, and moving into your new place all in one day!! That peace of mind is worth the rent you'll pay.

**Q. When should I start the process of downsizing?**

A. It's never too early to start. Begin today! There are companies that will downsize for you. They work with charitable organizations and estate sale companies to help you give away or sell your belongings. These firms will organize and pack for you, hire movers, and unpack on the other end. In short, they can help with the entire moving process.

Your family may wish to help with the move or claim some treasures before you get rid of them. Let them know your plans before you get rid of anything!

## Q. When do I have an estate sale?

A. Many of my clients find that the estate sale works best when timed between the accepted offer and the move-out date. If you've structured your move-out date to be after the closing date but while you're renting back from the buyer, you can move into your new apartment first, then have the estate sale. Otherwise, have the estate sale after you know the buyer has committed to purchasing your home (usually after the home inspection has been approved by your buyer, which is generally ten days after you've accepted their offer).

# RESOURCES

American Association of Retired Persons
**www.aarp.org**
Every issue facing seniors; legal, caregiving, lifestyle choices, etc.

American Home Shield (AHS)
**www.ahswarranty.com**                    **1-800-776-4663**
AHS provides comprehensive, affordable home warranty coverage and service on mechanical system failures while your home is on the market. This coverage can be extended by the new owner when the home is sold.

Angie's List
**www.angieslist.com**
Angie's list a word-of-mouth network for consumers looking for local service companies such as plumber, carpenters, roofers, etc.

Better Business Bureau (Wisconsin)
**www.bbb.org**                                **1-703-276-0100**
This organization promotes ethical business practices and public confidence through voluntary self-regulation, consumer and business education, and service excellence.

Council of Residential Specialists (CRS)
**www.crs.com**                                **1-800-462-8841**
The association was created to recruit and retain those realtors seeking the knowledge, tools, and relationship-building opportunities needed to maximize their professionalism in residential real estate.

The CRS designation recognizes professional accomplishments in both experience and education and is the highest designation awarded to sales associates in the residential sales field.

The Elder Care Locator
**www.eldercare.gov**                          **1-800-677-1116**
The Eldercare Locator is designed to help older adults and their families and caregivers find their way through the maze of services for seniors by identifying trustworthy local support resources. The goal is to provide users with the information and resources they need that will help older persons live independently and safely in their homes and communities for as long as possible.

Dr. Randy O. Frost, Ph. D.
**rfrost@smith.edu**
Articles and information regarding compulsive hoarding (collecting/saving items taken to extreme).

Home Security of America (HAS)
**www.onlinehsa.com**                          **1-800-367-1448**
This company provides comprehensive, affordable home warranty coverage and service on mechanical system failures while

your home is on the market. Coverage can be extended by the new owner when the home is sold.

National Association of Senior Move Managers (NASMM)
**www.nasmm.com**
NSAMM is a nonprofit, professional association of organizations dedicated to helping older adults and their families with the physical and emotional aspects of moving. Members are committed to maximizing the dignity and autonomy of older adults as they transition from one living environment to another.

New LifeStyles Online
**www.newlifestyles.com**          **1-800-869-9549**
New Lifestyles Online is the ultimate resource for senior living and care options. This site provides you with everything you need to make an informed, comfortable decision about your own or your loved one's future. Extensive resources are easily accessible, which not only saves you time and money, but helps cut down on the frustration of trying to find information from multiple sources, agencies, or organizations.

Whether you are looking for an Independent Retirement Community, Assisted Living Facilities, Senior Housing, Nursing Home, Alzheimer's Care, Home or Hospice Care, or other senior product or senior service, New LifeStyles Online can help you find what's right for you.

The Senior Advantage Real Estate Council (SAREC)
**www.seniorsrealestate.com**          **1-800-500-4564**
Senior Real Estate Specialist (SRES) are realtors qualified to meet the special needs and concerns of maturing Americans. They have completed the necessary educational program and demonstrate the knowledge and expertise to counsel senior clients through major financial and lifestyle transitions involved in relocating, refinancing, or selling the family home.

Senior Law Home Page
**www.seniorlaw.com**　　　　　　**212-387-8400/914-397-0900**
This is a Web site where senior citizens, their families, attorneys, social workers, and financial planners can access information about elder law, Medicare, Medicaid, guardianship, estate planning, trusts, and the rights of the elderly and disabled.

Society of Certified Senior Advisors (CSA)
**www.society-csa.com**　　　　　　**1-800-653-1785**
CSAs understand how to build effective relationships with seniors because the CSA education has given them a broad-based knowledge of the health, social, and financial issues that are important to seniors, along with the dynamics of how these factors work together in seniors' lives. The Society of Certified Senior Advisors teaches professionals what's important to seniors and how – always – to put their clients' interests first.

# Bruce Nemovitz
## Helping to design the best years of your life

**www.BrucesTeam.com**

**Give Me A Call: 262-242-6177**

Bruce can be contacted at 262 242-6177 or you may email Bruce at **bruce@brucesteam.com**.

Please contact Bruce directly for quantity discounts or to inquire about his availability to speak to your group.

Also see **movingintherightdirectionbook.com**.

Made in the USA
Columbia, SC
06 December 2022

72435159R00054